250

Glenn E

MODERN AMERICAN WRITERS

IV. H. L. MENCKEN

H. L. MENCKEN

By
ERNEST BOYD

ROBERT M. McBRIDE & COMPANY
NEW YORK :: :: :: :: :: :: 1925

CONTENTS

H. L. MENCKEN

THE AMERICAN

ONE of the most extraordinary legends in American literature is the legend that there is a legendary H. L. Mencken. When an author creates for himself a fictitious literary personality, as Bernard Shaw has done, it is usually in order to conceal the discrepancy between his real self and the image which his writings have formed in the mind of the public. Mr. Shaw is not a picturesque rebel, meditating the destruction of capitalistic society; an iconoclast absorbed in the struggle for democracy and freedom. He is a hard-headed business man, who has become a highly paid purveyor of popular amusement; an unattached Irishman in London making a career out of attacking English conventions which were never his own. His Socialism at an early stage resolved itself into the statistics of Mr. and Mrs. Sidney Webb and the Fabians, and his predilection for orthodox society has kept him immune from the heretical ideas and personalities that have effected such changes as he professes theoretically to be interested in, whether it be the achievement of self-government in Ireland, or the overthrow of capitalist government in Russia. The legendary G.B.S. is obviously a fiction essential to the success of George Bernard Shaw.

Henry Louis Mencken, on the contrary, requires no legend, for he is as authentically himself in his writings as was Anatole France. He writes as he speaks, and his most casual conversation or letter differs in no way from his most formal or elaborate essays. He is vigorous, boisterous and Rabelaisian; good-humored and intolerant of humbug; a libertarian and an immoralist; a hedonist, but of the simplest tastes; he is a naturally irreligious, irreverent, easy-going, individualist, wholly without sentiment where his interests are involved, and convinced that self-help and self-reliance are all that one requires to succeed. There is not an aspect of his character which is not reflected in his writings, and not an element in the Mencken legend which has not been derived from them. The man and the legend are one, and conjointly they present the inspiring and fascinating spectacle of a real American, as distinct from the modern ex-European substitute, known as a one hundred per cent. American. In America he lives, moves and has his being, less troubled by alien ideas and interests than any other prominent publicist in the United States to-day. The American scene holds and absorbs all his energies, and reversing the common order of things, he sees in Europe merely a remote territory where inferior Americans go:

"I remain on the dock, wrapped in the flag, when the Young Intellectuals set sail . . . Here I stand, unshaken and undespairing, a loyal and devoted Americano, even a chauvinist, paying taxes without complaint, obeying all laws that are physiologically obeyable, accepting all the searching duties and responsibilities of citizenship unprotestingly, investing the sparse usufructs of my miserable toil in the obligations of the nation, avoiding all commerce with men sworn to overthrow the government, contributing my mite toward the glory of the national arts and sciences, enriching and embellishing the native language, spurning all lures (and even all invitations) to get out and stay out—here am I, a bachelor of easy means, forty-two years old, unhampered by debts or issue, able to go wherever I please and to stay as long as I please—here am I, contentedly and even smugly basking beneath the Stars and Stripes, a better citizen, I daresay, and certainly a less murmurous and exigent one, than thousands who put the Hon. Warren Gamaliel Harding beside Friedrich Barbarossa and Charlemagne, and hold the Supreme Court to be directly inspired by the Holy Spirit. . . ."

It is characteristic of this attachment of his to his own country that his patriotism takes the extreme form of parochialism. He was born in Baltimore, Maryland, forty-five years ago, and has lived there ever since—for forty-two years of the time actually in the same house. His local pride is con-

siderable, and his attitude towards New York is one
of mingled hostility and contempt. He views that
thronged, ever-changing cosmopolitan scene with the
provincial patriot's deep conviction that such a
metropolis is fundamentally incompatible with the
aims and character of American civilization. He
speaks of the "glittering swinishness" of this Bab-
ylon, and there is a note of warning in his statement
that "what is in vogue among the profiteers of Manhattan and their harlots to-day is imitated by the
flappers of the Bible Belt country clubs week after
next." He finds the atmosphere "grown increasingly levantine," and he declares that "the Paris of
the Second Empire pales to a sort of snobbish
Chautauqua; the New York of Ward McAllister becomes the scene of a convention of Gold Star
Mothers. To find a parallel for the grossness and
debauchery that now reign in New York one must
go back to the Constantinople of Basil I."

It was assuredly a wish that was father to the
thought which prompted Mr. Mencken to rationalize
his affection for the provinces—or rather their
equivalent in the United States—and to promulgate
the theory that Chicago not New York was the
literary capital of this country. The notion rested
on no more solid basis than the fact that few writers
in New York for a generation or more have been
native New Yorkers or have borne any stamp common
to that city. By the same test, of course, London
and Paris would equally fail to justify their ex-

istence as literary capitals, for there is no Parisian quality common to Paul Bourget and André Gide, nor has London established any identity between G. K. Chesterton and John Galsworthy. But in the five years since the theory was formulated almost every Chicagoan of note has settled in New York, and Mr. Mencken has formally pronounced his anathema upon the capital of the Middle West as the cradle of modern American literature. The essay is still valuable merely for the light it throws upon Mr. Mencken's fundamental antagonism to metropolitan life. Here in Menckenian form are the immemorial plaints of the small town against the city:

"Alone among the great cities of the world it has no definite intellectual life, no body of special ideals and opinions, no aristocratic attitudes, even the common marks of nationality are few and faint; one half wonders . . . if it is actually American at all. Huge, Philistine, self-centered, ignorant and vulgar, it is simply a sort of free port, a Hansa town, a place where the raw materials of civilization are received. . . . Life buzzes and coruscates on Manhattan Island, but the play of ideals is not there. The New York spirit, for all the gaudy pretentiousness of the town, is a spirit of timidity, of regularity, of safe mediocrity. . . . The town is shoddily cosmopolitan, second-rate European, extraordinarily cringing."

This distorted view of the life of New York is pe-

culiarly American, and is one to which no European
observer would subscribe, unless he were one of those
who hold that all capitals, as such, are unrepre-
sentative and deleterious in their effect upon the individuals whom they draw into their vortex.   Mr.
Mencken himself has eloquently depicted the South
as "the Sahara of the Bozart," and his remarks
about other cities do not recommend them as alter-
natives to New York.   Boston is "as tragically dead
as Alexandria and Padua"; Philadelphia is "an
intellectual slum"; Washington, St. Louis, New
Orleans and Baltimore are "simply degraded and
flabby villages."   As for San Francisco, "its old life
and color are gone, and the Methodists, Baptists and
other such vermin of God now dominate it."   From
which the impartial critic would conclude that there
was no good anywhere, but that Mr. Mencken particularly abominated the one city which has escaped
relatively the worst horrors of the evangelical provincialism which he has devoted his life to exposing
and ridiculing.

At all events, enough has been said to show that
it was no mere accident which kept H. L. Mencken
in Baltimore, and that his persistent predilection for
that somnolent town is an essential characteristic of
his authentic Americanism.   He was educated there,
graduated from the Baltimore Polytechnic at the age
of sixteen, and is "theoretically competent to run a
steam engine or a dynamo, but is actually quite in-
capable of doing either."   That year is further cele-

brated as the one in which he made his first appearance in print, a poem contributed to the Baltimore *American*, in 1896. By a happy chance, he did not submit to the standardizing process of a university education, and in 1899, after his father's death, he became a reporter on the Baltimore *Morning Herald*, where he wrote, amongst other things, his first column, "Knocks and Jollies," and a series of burlesques entitled "Untold Tales." In 1903, he became city editor and published his first book, the almost fabulous *Ventures into Verse*. By the time he was twenty-five he was managing editor and the author of *George Bernard Shaw: His Plays*, the earliest book in English on the subject and the only work of his nonage which he has not completely repudiated. For a brief period he was editor-in-chief of the *Evening Herald*, then news editor of the Baltimore *Evening News* until, in 1906, he joined the staff of the Baltimore *Sun*, serving in various capacities and forming the journalistic connection which was to enable him to develop into the unique force in the newspaper world from which his wider reputation evolved. In 1908 the *Evening Sun* was started and he was one of the editors, contributing a signed article on the editorial page, which in 1911 crystallized as the famous "Free Lance" column and continued until he resigned in 1915. Since then he has written at varying intervals for that paper, with which he has never wholly abandoned his connection. In fact, until the spring of 1925, when he commenced to syndicate a weekly article through the Chicago *Tribune*, the Baltimore *Evening Sun* was the only daily newspaper for which he wrote regularly.

It will be noted that this entire period of activity, from 1899 until 1916, was concentrated in Baltimore and, with one exception, Mr. Mencken's writings for publication outside his home town were of minor importance. Between 1899 and 1905 he had written verse for *The Bookman,* and for such magazines as *Leslie's Weekly* and *Life.* He was also a contributor of short stories at this time to the London *Idler, Short Stories, The Red Book,* and *Frank Leslie's Popular Monthly,* which was then edited by Mr. Ellery Sedgwick, who can claim to have been the first editor of note to discover the writer now regarded as the anti-Christ of New England culture. As a contributor to *The Delineator* in 1908, H. L. Mencken was brought into contact with Theodore Dreiser, a meeting which provided the new critic with a subject which was to be a scourge for the orthodox. Some of the verse of this period was collected in his first book, but the rest of his magazine writings are in the limbo of yellowing files.

The only place, apart from the Baltimore press, where Mr. Mencken wrote regularly during the years when he was building up his fame was in *The Smart Set,* where he began his monthly article on books in 1908, with George Jean Nathan as his associate in dramatic criticism. Six years later the two friends became editors and part owners of the magazine, and jointly created for themselves and *The Smart Set* a reputation in which all the qualities peculiar to Mr. Nathan were attributed to his partner, for the Mencken of legend is the Nathan of fact. While the Nietzschean blonde beast of the philistine imagination cultivated the domestic virtues with his mother and sister in their family home in Baltimore, George Jean Nathan effectively practiced the doctrine of sacred egoism in New York. The partnership was dissolved in July 1925, when Mr. Nathan withdrew from the editorial side of *The American Mercury*, which they had launched together in 1924, after having disposed of their interest in *The Smart Set*. The association had been long, fruitful, and, in its way, unique in American literature, for never were two men so dissimilar. It enabled Mr. Mencken to cultivate his Maryland garden while enjoying the notoriety of a life of gaudy pleasure and heresy quite alien to him. It enabled Mr. Nathan to consummate an attitude in which he has realized a personality. Neither could have carried on the magazine alone, for H. L. Mencken would not sacrifice the calm of his bourgeois existence for the Sodom and Gomorrah of Manhattan, and George Jean Nathan could never have achieved that patient, maieutic tenderness to young or struggling authors, upon which the advocate of Nietzschean hardness has lavished so many hours of a busy life.

H. L. Mencken, therefore, is as essentially of Baltimore as Ed. Howe and William Allen White are of Kansas, and his claim for the State of Maryland, that it is the "apex of normalcy," is in itself a significant commentary upon his devotion to what he calls—obviously in self-defense—"the Maryland Free State." Neither Mr. Howe nor Mr. White has ever been denounced as an emissary of the Evil One, just as Mr. Mencken has never been credited by his adversaries with the plain homely virtues, the qualities for which Americans profess a touching respect embodied in the phrase "just folks," which is the nearest equivalent in English to the German *gemüthlich*. Mr. Mencken is nothing if not *gemüthlich*, and his possible preference for this barbaric Teutonic vocable need not blind us to the real connotations of the word. Very naturally he elects, like the two prophets of provincialism already named, to live beyond the reach of that swirling current of raffish, disquieting modern life which foams through New York and sends its spray and the noise of its waters far back into the hinterland, throwing up in its course those problems which engage the terrorized attention of moralists and reformers.

"Maryland bulges with normalcy. Freed, by the providence of God, from the droughts and dervishes, the cyclones and circular insanities of the Middle West, and from the moldering doctrinairism and appalling bugaboos of the South, and from the biological decay of New England, and from the incurable corruption and menacing unrest of the other industrial States, it represents, in a sense, the ideal toward which the rest of the Republic is striving. It is safe, fat, and unconcerned. It can feed itself, and have plenty to spare. It drives a good trade, foreign and domestic; it makes a good profit; banks a fair share of it. It seldom freezes in winter, and it stops short of actual roasting in summer. It is bathed in a singular and various beauty, from the stately estuaries of the Chesapeake to the peaks of the Blue Ridge. It is unthreatened by floods, Tulsa riots, Non-partisan Leagues, Bolshevism, or Ku Klux Klans. . . . It has its own national hymn, and a flag older than the Stars and Stripes. It is the home of the oyster, of the deviled crab, of hog and hominy, of fried chicken *à la Maryland*. It has never gone dry. . . . I depict, you may say, Utopia, Elysium, the New Jerusalem. My own words, in fact, make me reel with State pride; another *Lis'l* of that capital moonshine *Löwenbrau*, and I'll mount the keg and begin bawling 'Maryland, My Maryland!' " The only defect in this Arcadia, it seems, is the advance of industrialism, which has obliterated the old aristocratic social lines based upon the ownership of land. Otherwise, this golden mean, now being reduced to "the dream paradise of every true Americano," would apparently leave Mr. Mencken undisturbed.

Whenever he is guilty of the slightest treason against Baltimore, he hastens to make amends, dismissing his own complaints as mere rhetoric. "The old charm still survives, despite the boomers, despite

the street-wideners, despite the forward lookers. . . .
I am never more conscious of it than when I return
to the city, after a week in New York. There is a
great city, huge, rich and eminent, and yet it has no
more charm than a circus lot or a jazzy hotel. . . .
I have confessed to rhetoric, but here I surely do not
indulge in it. For twenty-four years I have resisted
almost constant temptation to move to New York,
and I resist it more easily to-day than I did when it
began." This confession is not the usual urban
romanticism about the charms of country life, to
which intellectuals are so frequently addicted. Mr.
Mencken's conception of rustic simplicity, his view
of rural society, is as unsympathetic and hostile as
his attitude towards the metropolis. His despair
at the hegira of literary Chicago springs from a
deep-seated belief in the virtues of provincialism. If
he has his office on Manhattan Island, but resides in
Baltimore, it is not because he prefers to be awak-
ened at dawn by the shrill and exasperating vociferations of misguided birds, rather than to sleep peace-
fully to the soothing hum and roar of the city's
noises. It is because his fundamental instincts and
ideals are safeguarded in the small town—for, whatever census statistics and real estate agents may
say, Baltimore is quintessentially what Americans
mean by "small town," what Europeans call provincial. Provincialism is a state of mind.

Theodore Roosevelt crusading against "race
suicide," Ed Howe truculently urging the superi-

ority to Goethe of the leading realtor in Atchison, Kansas, the organizers of Mother's Day reducing family affection to terms of the goose-step, have not pleaded more eloquently for the sanctity of hearth and home. "What makes New York so dreadful, I believe, is mainly the fact that the vast majority of its people have been forced to rid themselves of one of the oldest and most powerful human instincts —the instinct to make a permanent home." The householder moves out of a house into a large apartment, then he is driven into a smaller one, abandoning most of his goods and chattels, and "finally he lands in a hotel. At this point he ceases to exist as the head of a house. . . . The front he presents to the world is simply an anonymous door on a gloomy corridor. Inside he lives like a sardine in a can." To such a habitation the sacred name of home cannot be applied, as Mr. Mencken points out in a passage of more sustained emotion than has ever crept into his diabolonian onslaughts upon the more superficial phenomena of American life:

"A home is not a mere transient shelter: its essence lies in its permanence, in its capacity for accretion and solidification, in its quality of representing, in all its details, the personalities of the people who live in it. In the course of years it becomes a sort of museum of those people; they give it its indefinable air, separating it from all other homes, as one human face is separated from all others. It is at once a refuge from the world, a treasure-house, a castle, and the shrine of a whole hierarchy of peculiarly private and potent gods.

"This concept of the home cannot survive the mode of life that prevails in New York. I have seen it go to pieces under my eyes in the houses of my own friends. The intense crowding in the town, and the restlessness and unhappiness that go with it, make it almost impossible for any one to accumulate the materials of a home—the trivial, fortuitous and often grotesque things that gather around a family, as glories and debts gather around a state. The charm of getting home, as I see it, is the charm of getting back to what is inextricably my own—to things familiar and long loved, to things that belong to me alone and none other. I have lived in one house for forty years. It has changed in that time, as I have—but somehow it still remains the same. No conceivable decorator's masterpiece could give me the same ease. It is as much a part of me as my two hands. If I had to leave it, I'd be as certainly crippled as if I lost both legs.

"I believe that this feeling for the hearth, for the immemorial lares and penates, is infinitely stronger here than in New York—that it has better survived here, indeed, than in any other large city of America —and that its persistence accounts for the superior charm of the town. There are, of course, thousands of Baltimoreans in flats—but I know of none to whom a flat seems more than a makeshift, a substitute, a necessary and temporary evil. They are all planning to get out, to find house-room in one of the new suburbs, to resume living in a home. What they see about them is too painfully not theirs. The New Yorker has simply lost that discontent. He is a vagabond. His notions of the agreeable become those of a vaudeville actor. He takes on the shallowness and unpleasantness of any other homeless man. He is highly sophisticated, and inordinately trashy.

"The fact explains the lack of charm that one finds in his town; the fact that the normal Baltimorean is almost his exact antithesis explains the charm that is here. Human relations, in such a place as this, tend to assume a solid permanence. A man's circle of friends becomes a sort of extension of his family circle. His contacts are with men and women who are rooted as he is. They are not moving all the time, and so they are not changing their friends all the time. Thus abiding relationships tend to be built up, and when fortune brings unexpected changes they survive those changes. The men I know and esteem in Baltimore are, on the whole, men I have known and esteemed a long while; even those who have come into my ken relatively lately seem likely to last. But of the men I knew best when I first began going to New York, twenty-five years ago, not one is a friend to-day. Of those I knew best ten years ago not six are friends to-day. The rest have got lost in the riot, and the friends of to-day, I sometimes fear, will get lost in the same way."

"In human relationships that are so casual there is

seldom any satisfaction. It is our fellows who make life endurable to us, and give it a purpose and a meaning; if our contacts with them are light and frivolous there is something lacking, and it is something of the very first importance. What I contend is that in Baltimore, under a slow-moving and cautious social organization, such contacts are more enduring than elsewhere, and that life in consequence is more charming. Of the external embellishments of life we have a plenty—as great a supply, indeed, to any rational taste, as New York itself. But we have something much better: we have a tradition of sound and comfortable living."

The legendary H. L. Mencken exists solely in the minds of his hostile critics and his least intelligent admirers, who have derived their impression of him from his opponents rather than from himself. It is not necessary, moreover, to know the man personally in order to see him as he really is, for he is self-explanatory, and he has actually drawn a more complete and intimate portrait of himself in the course of his writings than any of the Greenwich Village exhibitionists whose alcove and its adulteries are their only literary asset. In *Pistols for Two*, the curious may learn that he is "five feet, eight and a half inches in height, and weighs about 185 pounds. In 1915 he bulged up to 197 pounds. Then he took the Vance Thompson cure and reduced to 175, rebounding later. He has good eyes and a gentle mouth, but his nose is upset, his ears stick out too much, and he is shapeless and stoop-shouldered. One could not imagine him in the movies. He has strong and white, but irregular teeth. He wears a No. 7½ hat. He is bow-legged. He is a fast walker. He used to snore when asleep, but had his nasal septum straightened by surgery, and does so no longer. He wears B.V.D.'s all the year round, and actually takes a cold bath every day. He never has his nails manicured, but trims them with a jacknife. He wears Manhattan garters, No. 15½ Belmont collars, and very long-tailed overcoats. He works in his shirt-sleeves and sleeps in striped pajamas."

Almost every he-man in the United States will recognize in these personal details the sure and certain signs of a normalcy comparable only to that of the Maryland Free State itself. A Carlyle would have diagnosed these clothes from his works, or have divined his clothes and his habits from his ideas. Confirmation of all deductions from the writings of H. L. Mencken abounds in the impressions recorded of him by his friends. Thus Professor H. M. Parshley describes him in his native habitat—a picture which logically closes this sketch of his personality:

"Nordic, blond, and healthy, he writes scornfully of 'one-building universities' and 'poltroonish professors' under the eyes of his University of Leipsic ancestors (good Lutherans all), whose medieval portraits adorn the walls of the house in a charming Baltimore street where he lives blamelessly with his mother.

"He often dines with professors; he re-reads *Huckleberry Finn* at frequent intervals; he has a magnificent pre-war cellar, guarded by two large iron doors; he keeps three pet turtles in the back yard; he waxes sentimental over beer, Schubert, and five-o'clock tea *à deux;* he is accused of holding opinions identical with those proper to the man in the street because he fails to appreciate *vers libre* and expressionistic art in general; he considers vice crusaders inferior to their quarry, having had experience of both; he is secretly an eager student of biological textbooks; he wears blue serge, unpressed; his typewriting would disgrace a freshman in the High School of Commerce; and he judges political scientists and musicians by their reactions respectively to Roosevelt aud Johann Strauss.

"After a hard day's work of self-imposed labor, he reads through a book in a short evening and motors at midnight; or on occasion he entertains with genial conviviality a visiting pilgrim or two. Periodically he goes to discuss affairs and bodily infirmities with his trusty partner in New York, but he cannot work there. Aside from the conventions of the great political parties and journeys abroad, there is but one other interest that serves to mitigate the toilsome laboriousness of his life. He is presiding genius and second pianist of the Saturday Night Club, a small band of choice spirits (including select professors) devoted to the art of orchestral music, the pleasures of the table, and improving discourse.

To see him thus in company is finally to know him, for it is, perhaps, under such genial circumstances only, that the spirit of man can completely and beautifully unfold."

With this glimpse of a figure out of the golden age of American innocence, we may turn to the philosophical writings of H. L. Mencken. They are the complete reflection of that age, of the pre-Jacksonian period of capitalistic individualism.

THE PHILOSOPHER

I

THERE are a few glimpses of sardonic humor in *Ventures into Verse*, which might be regarded as evidence that the youth is father to the man. This little book is so rare, and it offers such opportunities for facetiousness, that its characteristics are now familiar through quotation on the part of innocents who enjoy the illusion that they alone have read the volume. It will be sufficient to say that Mr. Mencken's conception of poetry as an escape from thought, as a youthful flight from reality has at least the virtue of empiricism; it is not an *a priori* judgment, and it dispenses with the necessity of looking through his book for an early formulation of his philosophy. *Ventures into Verse* contains poems in the Kipling manner which are assuredly no worse than some of the *Barrack Room Ballads* and *Departmental Ditties*, but it differs from most youthful collections of the kind by its obvious lack of solemnity, from the title page to the closing refrain:

And the end of it all was a hole in the ground
And a scratch on a crumbling stone.

Sentiment, if it occurs, is appropriately punctured by cynicism, and a real sense of burlesque and of parody gives the book an interest which might not be suspected from the comments with which it has been favored by hostile professors. An eyewitness of the period declares that Mr. Mencken read a poem from the collection, and said: "I got twelve dollars for that, bought a hat and got drunk," to which came the obvious correction: "You mean, you got drunk and bought a hat"—an incident which sufficiently indicates the author's attitude towards his first book, whose preface was this "Preliminary Rebuke":

Gesundheit! Knockers! have your Fling!
Unto an Anvilfest you're bid;
It took a lot of Hammering,
To build Old Cheops' Pyramid!

"My early volume of dreadful verse got itself into type simply because two young fellows that I knew were setting up a printing-office and wanted a manuscript to exercise their art upon. They came to me for suggestions, and I naturally suggested a book of my own composition. They preferred verse to prose, and so verse it was." In this haphazard manner Mr. Mencken's first book was published, and the second, *George Bernard Shaw: His Plays*, came into existence almost as fortuitously. "Two years later, when Brentano began printing Shaw in America, I was greatly delighted by the format he gave to *The Quintessence of Ibsenism,* and decided forthwith to write a book on Shaw himself in the same form."

The author of the first book on Bernard Shaw was more concerned, very naturally, with exposition than with analysis, and Mr. Mencken's failure to reprint this work may be attributed largely to the fact that the lapse of twenty years has rendered it superfluous. It is by no means one of those pieces of *juvenilia* which every writer has upon his conscience and would prefer to deny, if that were possible. The book has the contemporary value and the subsequent interest attaching to all pioneering work. If we no longer need these intelligent and succinct accounts of Shaw's plays and novels, we can recognize that, within the limits set for him. Mr. Mencken has not been surpassed, and rarely superseded, by the later commentators. In the considerable library of Shavian biography and exegesis, from Mr. Mencken's immediate successor in England, Holbrook Jackson, in 1907, down to J. S. Collis in 1925, and including Julius Bab, G. K. Chesterton, Charles Cestre, Augustin Hamon, H. C. Duffin, Joseph McCabe, Renée Deacon, Harold Owen, Herbert Skimpole, John Palmer, Richard Burton, and Archibald Henderson, the official Biographer—only M. Cestre and Mr. McCabe have seen Shaw in a perspective which it was not possible to obtain when Mr. Mencken first surveyed the field.

In the evolution of H. L. Mencken, his first critical

work has the significance of its choice of subject, at a time when it was as impossible for a young man susceptible to ideas not to be attracted to Shaw as it was inconceivable that the orthodox should be aware of his existence. Mr. Mencken had his attack of Shavianitis at the appropriate age, when there was some merit in "discovering" Shaw, and before it was too late either to escape the obvious or to recover from the generous illusions of one's critical nonage. That recovery is recorded in *Prejudices: First Series* where, having confessed to the pleasure still to be derived from Shaw's "great zest and skill" in "the fine art of exhibiting the obvious in unexpected and terrifying lights," of announcing "the obvious in terms of the scandalous," Mr. Mencken points out that he has never found in Shaw's works an original idea, "never a single statement of fact or opinion that was not anteriorly familiar, and almost a commonplace." Finally, he dismisses him as a pseudo-heretic, because "life to him is not a poem, but a series of police regulations. . . . Beauty is a lewdness, redeemable only in the service of morality. . . . Always the ethical obsession, the hall-mark of the Scotch Puritan, is visible in him. His politics is mere moral indignation. His esthetic theory is cannibalism upon esthetics." Such is the matured expression of the idea stated away back in 1905, when Mr. Mencken wrote of Shaw: "either he is exhibiting a virtue as a vice in disguise, or exhibiting a vice as a virtue in vice's clothing."

Thus the curve of one's chavianism is properly closed, but there still remains an aspect of that early work which is an expression of Mr. Mencken himself, and whose validity remains unaltered to this day. As the passage is the first illustration of what has since become familiar as the typical Menckenian style, it may be quoted in full. He points out how the century which included the birth of Darwinism determined the destiny of Bernard Shaw, as it would have altered the destiny of Napoleon. Then he proceeds to this characteristic confession of faith:

"Darwin is dead now, and the public that reads the newspapers remembers him only as the person who first publicly noted the fact that men look a good deal like monkeys. But his soul goes marching on. . . . From him, through Huxley, we have appendicitis, the seedless orange, and our affable indifference to hell. Through Spencer, in like manner, we have Nietzsche, Sudermann, Hauptmann, Ibsen, our annual carnivals of catechetical revision, the stampede for church union, and the aforesaid George Bernard Shaw. . . . Before Darwin gave the world 'The Origin of Species,' the fight against orthodoxy, custom, and authority was perennially and necessarily a losing one. On the side of the defense were ignorance, antiquity, piety, organization and respectability—twelve-inch, wire-wound, rapid-fire guns, all of them. In the hands of the scattered, half-hearted, unorganized, attacking parties there were but two weapons—the blow-pipe of impious doubt and the bludgeon of sacrilege. Neither, unsupported, was very effective. Voltaire, who tried both, scared the defenders a bit, and for a while there was a great pother and scurrying about, but when the smoke cleared away, the walls were just as strong as before and the drawbridge was still up. One had to believe or be damned. There was no compromise and no middle ground.

"And so, when Darwin bobbed up, armed with a new-fangled dynamite gun that hurled shells charged with a new shrapnel—facts—the defenders laughed at the novel weapon and looked forward to slaying its bearer. Spencer, because he ventured to question Genesis, lost his best friend. Huxley, for an incautious utterance, was barred from the University of Oxford. And then of a sudden there was a deafening roar and a blinding flash—and down went the walls. Ramparts of authority that had resisted doubts fell like hedge-rows before facts, and there began an intellectual reign of terror that swept like a whirlwind through Europe, America, Asia, Africa and Oceania. For six thousand years it had been necessary, in defending a doctrine, to show only that it was respectable or sacred. Since 1859 it has been needful to prove its truth."

Here, in characteristic phrase, is Mr. Mencken's philosophical exordium, the starting point not only of his survey of Shaw, but of his own philosophy. He is one of the few Americans who still pay public homage to Huxley, and his mechanistic agnosticism, coupled with his refractoriness to all authority which is merely "respectable or sacred," his instinctive challenge to all dogmas, other than those which are scientific, are essential factors in his nineteenth century rationalism. That he should proceed from this to Nietzsche was an inevitable transition, and in the Introduction to *The Philosophy of Friedrich Nietzsche* one is not surprised to find him linking the names of his masters in a sentence which sums up the aim, as it reveals the genesis, of that book. "It is high time," he writes, "for the race of Darwin and Huxley to know Nietzsche better," for "he has colored the thought and literature, the speculation and theorizing, the politics and superstition of the time." Nietzsche also challenges what is merely "respectable or sacred," and widens the breach made by the Victorian freethinkers. "Stripping an idea of its holiness and romance, its antiquity and authority, he burrows down into the heart of it and tries to estimate it in terms of its actual probability and reasonableness. That a thing is sacred or venerable or ancient or beautiful, does not interest him. The question is asked invariably, Is it true? If he concludes that it is not, he says so, and if it happens to be something that is regarded with unusual reverence by the majority of men—which means something whose inviolability is accepted without inquiry or the shadow of doubt—he says so with unusual heat and clamor."

Such is the Nietzsche whom H. L. Mencken set out

to explain and expound to the average reader in the
year 1908, when only five volumes of the German
philosopher's works had been translated into English, and there was no help for those "at sea in German and unfamiliar with the technicalities of the
seminaries." In the Preface to the third edition the
author looks back upon the rapid success of his
work, for it was rather well received by the reviewers,
even in England. Despite the refined shudders of
The Spectator at Mr. Mencken's journalistic style,
critics like W. L. Courtney greeted the book in
terms which are as favorable as any currently be-
stowed upon him by British critics, most of whom, to
this day, are obviously puzzled and shocked by his
manner of writing. The curious may turn to that
dreadfully named but actually quite readable volume
of essays by W. L. Courtney, *Rosemary's Letter-
Book* (1909), for the first English work in which
Mr. Mencken is discussed. Tradition also alleges
that the earliest appreciation of him by an American
critic of standing came from the pen of Professor
Brander Matthews.

Mr. Mencken's second book of prose, like the first,
is essentially a work of exposition, but it is *his*
Nietzsche rather than Nietzsche whom he expounds,
a philosophy which might be described as evolutionary or selective utilitarianism, with its roots in
Darwinism, but representing a step further than
the democratic humanitarianism of Bentham and
the English Positivists. The mysticism of Nietzsche

plays little part in Mr. Mencken's conception of him. The superman, in his interpretation, is a simpler figure than that which Nietzsche conceived, first as a Romantic genius, then as a Darwinian super-species, and finally as a racial type. Nietzsche's Romanticism, which has been so brilliantly analyzed by Baron Ernest Seillère, is not considered, nor is Seillère's book, the most important French study of Nietzsche, listed in the otherwise representative bibliography. The connection between Nietzschean individualism and Rousseauism is ignored, and stress is laid chiefly upon the iconoclasm of the German thinker. Nietzsche "the Crucified," the man of Mr. Mencken's abhorred "Messianic delusion," the Dyonisian mystic preaching a return to Nature, Nietzsche the ascetic,—these aspects of his subject do not interest the idol-smasher. The latter's concern is to show how Nietzsche's teaching "leads to a rejection of Christianity and democracy; how it points to a possible evolution of the human race through the immoralists to the superman; how it combats the majority of the ideas held holy and impeccable by mankind to-day."

That all of these promises are fulfilled in the course of the book does not mean that Mr. Mencken did violence to his author, but it does mean that he did not do full justice to his subject. Another exegetist might show that, of these three points, the "rejection of Christianity and democracy" alone tallies with Mr. Mencken's own teaching. He might further prove that an almost equal number of ideas held as reasonably sound (if not "holy and impeccable") by Mr. Mencken, were combated by Nietzsche. The "Messianic delusion" of the superman, with its hypothesis that high-caste men, unlike poets, are not born, but are made by circumstance; the belief that alcohol is a scourge; the Christian asceticism of the Dyonisian disciples who must "suffer pain, loneliness, sickness, scorn and degradation" to be worthy of the master—these are not precisely to be numbered amongst Mr. Mencken's dearest convictions. In the vast extent and variety of Nietzsche's writings there are texts to suit many purposes. Nothing could be more natural than that this particular commentator, at that particular time, should emphasize that element in Nietzsche's work which best fitted both his purpose and his own temperament. H. L. Mencken created Nietzsche in his own image, hence the affecting superstition that he is a Nietzschean.

This superstition is shared in America by his admirers and opponents alike, but only in an extremely limited sense can the term be applied to him. He is the author of a standard book on Nietzsche, he has translated *The Antichrist*, and he has defended its author, even to the point of declaring him, during the war, "The Prophet of the Mailed Fist," thereby differentiating himself from all other English-speaking Nietzscheans, including Dr. Oscar Levy, editor, translator and leader of the cult in England. He is a Nietzschean, in short, very much as many people are described—or describe themselves—as Christians, not because they practice the religion of Christ, or even believe in it, but because they have had a Christian education. Mr. Mencken has had a Nietzschean education, and he is loyal to his old teacher, but his philosophy of life and art has little of Nietzsche in it, and their points of contact are probably fewer than their points of divergence. Their one fundamental point of agreement is their rejection of Christianity and democracy, and this, it so happens, is the most obvious and striking feature of Nietzsche's philosophy, beyond which the general public has never penetrated to the heart of his system.

Nietzsche's criticism of Christianity is not original, except in its excessive animosity. The antidote is as old as the poison, and with the rise of Rousseau and Romanticism, it was revived in new forms as part of the general movement to sap the basis of existing society. What the Romantics called "the rights of passion," and our contemporary bohemians call "paganism," is nothing but this revolt against the morality of Christianity. It was Heine, however, not Nietzsche, who found in Hellenism a ready-made antithesis to Christian asceticism, and who declared himself a Greek by affinity, repudiating Nazarenes, both Jewish and Gentile. In his Wagnerian period, Nietzsche loathed the irony of Heine, so fatal to Dionysian mysticism, as to all other kinds, but, after the break with Wagner, he greeted him as "a European event," and the antithesis between Hellenic and Christian, of which he had not a word to say in *The Birth of Tragedy*, became the *Leitmotiv* of his later years. Allied to his anti-Christian was his anti-democratic attitude, for democracy was inevitably a consequence and an inseparable part of the morality he was attacking. He never learned to distinguish the forms of democracy, and denounced with the same arguments systems as contradictory as anarchism and collectivism.

To his criticism of Christianity and democracy Mr. Mencken owes his reputation as a Nietzschean, and towards democracy, at least, his attitude is characteristically so. In all that he has written on the subject, the reader will look in vain for any recognition on his part of the various systems of democratic government whose partisans differ as fundamentally from each other as Mr. Mencken differs from those whom he classifies vaguely as "democrats." This indifference to definitions logically involves a refusal to differentiate between forms of "democracy" as dissimilar as those which exist to-day in the United States and in Soviet Russia, in England and in France, in Denmark and in Switzerland. All of these countries are "democratic," but even the three republics mentioned are confronted with conditions and problems which are by no means similar merely because all three elect a president and permit themselves the luxury of what is politely

called "representative" government. Mr. Mencken,
of course, being one of those authentic Americans
wholly absorbed in the affairs of his own country,
speaks primarily of democracy in the United States,
but within that geographical limitation there are
shades of meaning to the word of which he takes no
cognizance. He does not argue the merits of National Guilds as against the Coöperative Commonwealth; the radical difference between State Socialism and Communism does not concern him; Ramsay
MacDonald and Lenin, Bernard Shaw and Bryan,
President Poincaré and President Coolidge apparently look alike to him: they are all "democrats."

In other words, Mr. Mencken has never considered
the relation of economics to politics, and he does
not seem to be aware of the fact that political power
is conditioned and determined by economic power.
In 1910 Robert Rives La Monte and H. L. Mencken
published a series of letters, entitled *Men Versus the
Man,* which purported to be a debate on Socialism.
It is a remarkable work in many ways. It is probably the only debate of its kind in recent times where
the Conservative carried off all the honors. Mr.
Mencken's arguments for individualism had all the
agility and wit which, in the days of similar discus-
sion under the auspices of the London Fabian Society, were invariably the monopoly of George Bernard Shaw and the Fabian Socialists. Mr. La
Monte was certainly destined to confirm his opponent in the belief that Socialism was no creed for an

intelligent man. At no stage was the word "Socialism" ever defined, and it would be impossible to say
whether Mr. Mencken was being invited to subscribe
to the gospel of Marx or of Sidney Webb.

Whether Mr. Mencken would have come away with
some notion of the economic basis of politics, had
the debate been between Bernard Shaw and himself,
it is hard to say. If Mr. La Monte failed woefully
to present his case intelligently, at least he afforded
his opponent an opportunity of formulating his own
doctrine of individualism in a manner which makes
this book of the utmost importance to a proper understanding of H. L. Mencken. It is the first work
in which he comes forward, not to expound another
man's ideas, but to define and defend his personal
philosophy. Mr. Mencken has written many millions
of words on political and social topics in the Baltimore press and in *The American Mercury*, most of
them scattered beyond recall, some of them collected
in such volumes as *In Defence of Women* and in the
four series of *Prejudices*, which have been increasingly devoted to general rather than literary subjects. In *Men Versus the Man* will be found in
embryo all his essential ideas, the general viewpoint
from which he has since discussed specific political
or social problems and questions of the day.

Having been invited to become a convert to something vaguely Marxian called "Socialism," Mr.
Mencken retorted that he was an individualist, and
that he regarded Socialism as a menace to indi-

vidualism in so far as its aim was, not to assist the
first-rate man, but to enable the mass of men to survive by means of artificial aids, when their manifest
fate was to go under or to play a subordinate rôle.
"Progress then, as I see it, is to be measured by the
accuracy of man's knowledge of nature's forces. . . .
I conceive progress as a sort of process of disil-
lusion. Man gets ahead, in other words, by discard-
ing the theory of to-day for the fact of to-morrow.
. . . The mob is inert and moves ahead only when it
is dragged or driven. It clings to its delusions with
a pertinacity that is appalling. A geological epoch
is required to rid it of a single error, and it is so
helpless and cowardly that every fresh boon it re-
ceives . . . must come to it as a free gift from its
betters—as a gift not only free but forced. Great
men have fought for the truth for a thousand years,
and yet the average low-caste white man of to-day
. . . still believes that Friday is an unlucky day,
still believes that ghosts walk the earth, and still
holds to an immovable faith in signs, portents, resur-
rections, redemptions, miracles, prophecies, hells,
gehennas, and political panaceas."

"What virtues do I demand in the man who claims
enrollment in the highest caste? Briefly, I demand
that he possess, to an unusual and striking degree,
all of those qualities, or most of them, which most
obviously distinguish the average man from the
baboon. . . . The chief of those qualities is a sort
of restless impatience with things as they are—a

sort of insatiable desire to help along the evolutionary process. The man who possesses this quality is ceaselessly eager to increase and fortify his mastery of his environment. He has a vast curiosity and a vast passion for solving the problems it unfolds before him. . . ."

"And so I arrive at my definition of the first-caste man. He is one whose work in the world increases, to some measurable extent, that everwidening gap which separates civilized man from the protozoan in the sea ooze. It is possible, you will note, for a man to amass billions, and yet lend no hand to this progress; and it is possible, again, for a man to live in poverty, and yet set the clock ahead a thousand years. It is possible once more, for a man to aid progress in one way and aid reaction in some other way. And so, to sum up, it is possible for a poor man to belong to the highest caste of men, and for a rich man to belong to the lowest; and it is possible, again, for one and the same man to belong, at different times or even at the same time, to both castes. . . . Let me cite John D. Rockefeller as an example. His vast improvements in the interchange of commodities entitle him to a place in the front rank of those whose lives have made for human progress; and yet his belief, as a good Baptist, that total immersion in water is a necessary prerequisite for entry into heaven, places him, quite unmistakably, in the lowest caste of superstitious barbarians. . . ."

"Castes are not made by man, but by nature.

They will be inevitable so long as every genus of living beings in the world is divided into species, and every species is made up of individuals whose resemblance to one another, however close it may be, never reaches identity. It is this variation which makes progress possible, for it gives certain individuals an advantage in the struggle for existence, and these individuals tend to crowd out their weaker brothers, and to make their own heartier qualities dominant in the general racial strain. . . . But Professor Ward dissents. He holds that 'class distinctions in society are wholly artificial, depend entirely upon environing conditions, and are in no sense due to differences in native capacity. . . .'

"This theory . . . is the favorite fallacy and chief solace of all degenerate and inefficient races of men. . . . It is one of the multitude of sophistries that meet the pragmatic test of truth, for it plainly makes life more bearable. The man who formulates it enjoys a comforting glow of relief, of conscious virtue, of martyrdom. He has found a scapegoat to bear the blame for his inability to rise above the morass in which he wallows, and that scapegoat he variously denominates fate, luck, civilization, plutocracy, privilege, the protective tariff, civil service reform, or the devil. . . . The great objections to Socialism, as a philosophy, are that it encourages and aggravates the feeling of martyrdom which burns in the breasts of all such incompetents, and that it inflames them, at the same time, with the idea that their discomfort is due, not to the operation of natural laws, which benefit the world by ridding it automatically and harshly of the unfit, but to the deliberate and devilish cruelty of their betters.

"That the commercial idea will rule mankind forever, I by no means assert. . . . It is constantly conditioned and modified by lesser concepts, any or all of which may one day conquer it. The military idea, for example, often rises to rivalry with it. For a few brief weeks in the summer of 1898 most Americans envied Dewey more than Rockefeller, and thought him a more useful and honorable citizen. . . . My own private view (the child, I must admit, of a very ardent wish) is that the idea of truth-seeking will one day take the place of the idea of money-making. That is to say, I believe that the Huxleys and Behrings of the world will one day loom up, in the eye of the race, as greater heroes than the St. Pauls and Augustines, the William Conquerors and Alexanders, the Rockefellers, Cecil Rhodeses, Krupps and Morgans. But that day is far distant. As yet there is scarcely a sign of its dawn. . . ."

"In order that the human race may go forward, it seems to me desirable that the rewards of extraordinary efficiency should be magnificently alluring, and that the penalties of complete inefficiency should be swift, merciless and terrible. It is not sufficient that unusual man be given enough to eat, and a roof to shelter him from the weather, for such things are within easy reach of practically all men.

. . . If he wants money, let him have money. If he wants power, honor, glory, worship, let him have what he wants. Perhaps that incomparable—but to the common man, incomprehensible—joy which comes with the consciousness of work well done, will suffice him. Perhaps, on the contrary, he will demand, not only riches for himself, but also guarantee that his children shall be rich for generations. Whatever he desires, he proves title to it by getting it."

"The men of less efficiency make a less splendid bargain, for the things that he offers for sale have less value. . . . It seems to me this is an admirable arrangement. If I had the power to change it, I should not make the slightest alteration. If I were told off to create a universe, I should adopt the whole plan bodily. . . . This scheme of things, whatever its horrors, at least makes for progress. . . . I am not a religious man, but I cannot think upon my own good fortune in life without a feeling that my thanks should go forth, somewhere and to some one. Wealth and eminence and power are beyond my poor strength and skill, but on the side of sheer chance I am favored beyond all comparison. My day's work is not an affliction, but a pleasure; my labor, selling in the open market, brings me the comforts that I desire; I am assured against all but a remote danger of starvation in my old age. Outside my window, in the street, a man labors in the rain with pick and shovel, and his reward is merely a roof for to-night and to-morrow's three meals. Contemplating the difference between his luck and mine, I cannot fail to wonder at the eternal meaninglessness of life. I wonder thus and pity his lot, and then, after a while, perhaps, I begin to reflect that in many ways he is probably luckier than I.

"But I wouldn't change places with him."

II

The fifteen years which have elapsed since H. L. Mencken declared the main tenets of his individualist creed have not witnessed any serious modification of their essentials. These years have seen the application of those beliefs to a criticism of contemporary American life which has earned for the author a reputation as the foremost publicist of his time. In 1911 Mr. Mencken started his "Free Lance" column in the Baltimore *Evening Sun*, where he was able to comment freely upon current affairs from the standpoint of a philosophy whose gist was to be found in *Men Versus the Man*. Those who followed that column, in the days of his purely local celebrity, when his other writings were few and read by a small but enthusiastic circle, can testify to the courage and vigor with which he applied to specific and concrete problems the test of his own uncompromising philosophy. Alone of its kind, the Free Lance column justified the existence of that peculiar type of American journalism, so incomprehensible to the

European mind and—significantly—eschewed by the one first-rate newspaper in the United States.

The Free Lance was not engaged in reporting the puns of his friends at lunch, or re-writing publicity notes, or announcing the death of Queen Anne. He realized what is presumably the theoretical purpose of the "column," namely to allow a writer to give full play to his personal ideas. H. L. Mencken, fortunately, had a personality, and the consequence was that his column became a remarkable phenomenon, as contrary to Upton Sinclair's theories about the slavery of the American press as to the popular conception of the function of the "colyumist," as a glorified combination of press-agent and society reporter. As might be expected, he invariably wrote in direct opposition to the conventional views of his paper, and actually engaged in direct controversy with its editorials. He reversed all the natural laws of the species by devoting most of his space to his opponents and by never advertising his personal friends.

In a private letter written after he had resigned his column, in the autumn of 1915, Mr. Mencken summed up, in terms as characteristic as they are authentic, the results of his activities:

"General aim: to combat, chiefly by ridicule, American piety, stupidity, tin-pot morality, cheap chauvinism in all their forms. Attacked moralists, progressives, boomers, patriots, reformers, and finally Methodists, etc., by name.

"Defended alcohol, regulated prostitution, Sunday sports, vivisection, war, etc. Often tackled osteopathy, Christian Science, direct primary, single tax, socialism.

"Invented many new words and terms, e.g., chemical purity, osseocaput, baltimoralist, smuthound, honorary pallbearer, snoutery, Boy Scout, snoutism, snouteuse, boozehound, malignant, morality,—some of which got into circulation.

"Supported women suffrage on ground that it would more quickly reduce democracy to an absurdity. Advocated $1 a day tax on bachelors on the ground that it is worth $1 a day to be free. Advocated armed resistance by city of Baltimore to tax exactions of the counties. Also, armed resistance to prohibition and Sabbatarianism. Offered prizes for the worst platitudes of the week—such things as a hair from the whiskers of Lyman Abbott, a can of vaseline, a map of the areas in Germany conquered by England, etc.

"*Defeated in all campaigns*—for regulating vice, for Continental Sunday, for neutrality in the war, against direct primary, etc.

"Drew up and urged passage of a law legalizing the assassination of public officials. Also, one licensing and regulating uplifters.

"Wrote, in all, about 2,000,000 words. Attacked in probably 10,000 letters to the editor. Resolutions passed against me by all religious and uplifting organizations save Catholic and Jewish."

The combination here of iconoclastic individualism and the wildest American burlesque humor is the quintessence of H. L. Mencken, and, as his wider public of to-day will recognize, the Free Lance column was a microcosm of his more familiar writings, whether they be his editorials in *The American Mercury* or the essays in *Prejudices*. Out of those experiences came the department of *Americana*, that compendium of national imbecility, and from his multiple contacts with all forms of American endeavor, ridiculous and sublime alike, comes that amazing allusiveness, that variety of knowledge, that rich incongruity of striking reference and metaphor which lend an endless charm and vividness to his variations upon a single theme: the incurable idiocy of the mass of men.

Having noted an early and general statement of that conviction, one can still turn with interest to its latest expression in *Prejudices: Fourth Series*.

"It is . . . one of my firmest and most sacred beliefs . . . that the government of the United States, in both its legislative arm and its executive arm, is ignorant, incompetent, corrupt, and disgusting. . . . It is another that the foreign policy of the United States . . . is hypocritical, disingenuous, knavish and dishonorable. . . . And it is my fourth (and, to avoid too depressing a bill, final) conviction that the American people, taking one with another, constitute the most timorous, sniveling, poltroonish, ignominious mob of serfs and goose-

steppers ever gathered under one flag in Christen-
dom since the end of the Middle Ages, and that they
grow more timorous, more sniveling, more poltroonish, more ignominious every day. . . . All of which
may be boiled down to this: that the United States
is essentially a commonwealth of third-rate men—
that distinction is easy here because the general level
of culture, of information, of taste and judgment,
of ordinary competence is so low. . . . Third-rate
men, of course, exist in all countries, but it is only
here that they are in public control of the state, and
with it of all the national standards."

If this passage be analyzed it will be found that
it is based upon the major premise of *Men Versus
the Man*, to wit, that the aim of civilization is to
develop individuals, not to coddle the mob, and that
America has reversed that aim. From that follows
all the consequences so forcibly summed up by Mr.
Mencken, and to each adjective might be appended
an essay of his, illustrating its aptness by reference
to some existing American phenomenon. Only a few
months ago he was called upon by the Baltimore *Sun*
to report the antics of an ex-Secretary of State who
went to Dayton, Tennessee, and announced that
Darwinism would be abolished in this country, like
liquor, by a constitutional Amendment. Many
people regard these bursts of Menckenian eloquence
and vituperation either as entertaining exercises in
rhetoric or as coarse exhibitions of bad taste. Mr.
Mencken's constant preoccupation with the excesses

of puritanism and mobocracy seems to English readers to be entirely a work of supererogation. It is impossible for outsiders to understand the *actualité*, day in day out, of his subjects and his comments thereon. The fact is, however, that every point in his indictments is based upon some tangible fact of American life, however grotesque the hyperbole of his statement.

H. L. Mencken's taste has been questioned and his aims have been denounced, but the occasions when his facts have been challenged are exceedingly rare. It is the form of his criticism which has misled his opponents, as it has undoubtedly established his fame. Had he, for example, discussd his theory that the United States is "a commonwealth of third-rate men" in terms of the higher Ku Klux Kriticism, his contentions would have aroused the same sympathetic interest as those of Professor Wilbur C. Abbott in *The New Barbarians*, Professor McDougall in *The Indestructible Union*, or any of the hundred and one prophets of the Nordic myth. To the impartial eye all are alike in their concern for what they regard as the deterioration of American society. "The truth is that the majority of non-Anglo-Saxon immigrants since the Revolution, like the majority of Anglo-Saxon immigrants before the Revolution, have been, not the superior men of their native lands, but the botched and unfit: Irishmen starving to death in Ireland, Germans unable to weather *The Sturm und Drang* of the post-Napoleonic reorganization, Italians weed-grown on exhausted soil, Scandinavians run to all bone and no brain, Jews too incompetent to swindle even the barbarous peasants of Russia, Poland and Roumania."

These words were not written in the academic shades of New England, but are from the already quoted essay "On Being an American" in the last volume of *Prejudices*. Except for their absence of racial and patriotic superstition, they are identical in their implications with all that has been said by American sociologists and students of history in recent years. Restriction of immigration is their logical sequel, but the advantage of Mr. Mencken's logic involves a different test of desirability in the alien. Mr. Mencken agrees with all intelligent observers that, somehow or other, the United States are not what they used to be. His remedy, if he were to suggest one, would tally completely with his general view of life, and would differ thereby from the professions, if not the actual beliefs, of his contemporaries, but his diagnosis of the American malady is the same as theirs.

"The Fathers of the Republic, I am convinced, had a great deal more prevision than even their most romantic worshipers give them credit for. They not only sought to create a governmental machine that would be safe from attack without; they also sought to create one that would be safe from attack within. They invented very ingenious devices for holding the mob in check, for protecting the national polity against its transient and illogical rages, for securing the determination of all the larger matters of state to a concealed but none the less real aristocracy. Nothing could have been further from the intent of Washington, Hamilton and even Jefferson than that the official doctrines of the nation, in the year 1922, should be identical with the nonsense heard in the chautauqua, from the evangelical pulpit, and on the stump. But Jackson and his merry men broke through the barbed wires thus so carefully strung, and ever since 1825 *vox populi* has been the true voice of the nation."

In thus voicing the dissatisfaction of "the civilized minority" with the trend of modern American life Mr. Mencken is more logical than those who criticize the existing state of affairs, but continue to pay homage to the shibboleths which are responsible for the evils in question. He does not do lip service to ideals which are wholly incompatible with modern conditions, and he does not, therefore, find himself in the dilemma of so many publicists and public men in the United States who stand—metaphorically speaking—with the Bill of Rights in one hand and a deportation order in the other. It is to this peculiar form of political ancestor worship that most of the absurdities may be traced upon which Mr. Mencken loves to descant. Other countries make no pretense of being havens of refuge for all friends of liberty, so that when they exclude or harass individuals for racial, political or religious reasons, they are not troubled by the ghost of the Declaration of Independence, and so can proceed about the business in a calm and dignified manner betokening an easy conscience. Where there is an excessive romantic and oratorical attachment to the abstract idea of Freedom, an almost morbid and hysterical fear lest it be exercised is a very natural practical consequence in a country like the United States.

Mr. Mencken, being a *Realpolitiker*, is perpetually aware of this discrepancy between theory and practice, and being, further, a superb journalist, he loses no opportunity of illustrating from current events this dichotomy and its resultant hypocrisies, phobias, hysterias and injustices. Uncle Sam has a Declaration of Independence complex, and it is H. L. Mencken's pleasure to trace the strange workings of this neurosis. In the existing circumstances this picturesque eighteenth-century yearning must be suppressed, but the patient, needless to say, is unaware of the form the repression has taken. The Baltimore analyst knows; he is not to be put off with pictures of the spirit of '76.

"What then, is the spirit of Americanism? I precipitate it conveniently into the doctrine that the way to ascertain the truth about anything, whether in the realms of exact knowledge, in the purple zone of the fine arts or in the empyrean reaches of metaphysics, is to take a vote upon it, and that the way to propagate that truth, once it has been ascertained and proclaimed by lawful authority, is with a club. This doctrine, it seems to me, explains almost everything that is indubitably American, and particularly everything American that is most puzzling to men of older and less inspired cultures. . . . At one end it explains the archetypical buffooneries of the Ku Klux Klan, the American Legion, the Anti-Saloon League, the Department of Justice and all other such great engines of cultural propaganda, and at the other end it explains the amusing theory that the limits of the nation's esthetic adventures are to be fixed by a vague and self-appointed camorra of rustic Ph.D.'s. . . ."

In the third volume of *Prejudices*, the essay on "The Nature of Liberty" is a sardonic elaboration of this theme, with special reference to the unprecedented power and insolence of the police in this country and their immunity from all practical control. The essay is comparable for its irony to Anatole France's celebrated testimony to the divine impartiality of the law, which arrests the poor man and the rich alike, if they are found sleeping under a bridge. The theme is one which incessantly inspires H. L. Mencken to caustic comment, for the regimentation of opinion has assuredly reached an astonishing degree of efficiency in the United States. If he dwells so frequently upon the national craving for parades and friendly orders, upon the fantastic efforts to regulate the street traffic, upon the trickeries and campaigns of self-appointed reform organizations, upon the thousand and one forms of serious and petty tyranny, from lynching bees to Mother's Day—it is because all of these things are symptoms of an increasingly sheep-like submission to suggestion, to commands and to the terrorization of mob pressure.

"A minority not only has no more inalienable rights in the United States; it is not even lawfully entitled to be heard. This was well established by the case of the Socialists elected to the New York Assembly. What the voters who elected these Socialists asked for was simply the privilege of choosing spokesmen to voice their doctrines in a perfectly lawful and peaceable manner,—nothing more. This privilege was denied them." The Supreme Court is the one place where the rights of the individual and of minorities might be upheld, but Mr. Mencken has pointed out in many articles how that Court has, in turn, succumbed to "the prevailing doctrine that the minority has no rights which the majority is bound to respect." He reiterates his contention, with proofs adduced, that "the old rights of the free American, so carefully laid down by the Bill of Rights, are now worth nothing. Bit by bit, Congress and the State Legislatures have invaded and nullified them, and to-day they are so flimsy that no lawyer not insane would attempt to defend his client by bringing them up. Imagine trying to defend a man denied the use of the mails by the Postmaster-General, without hearing or even formal notice, on the ground that the Constitution guarantees the right of free speech! The very catch-polls in the courtroom would snicker."

In this zeal for the rights of man H. L. Mencken has the theoretical support of every patriotic citizen in this great Republic. In his belief that those rights are invaded more and more each year he has the support of a more or less intelligent minority. Actually, however, he is alone, save for a handful of convinced supporters, because his criticism is based upon premises which few Americans share with him. It is always amusing to observe the strange allies who come to him, oblivious of this interesting and fundamental difference between him and them. He lists amongst "the things he dislikes most" *The Nation* and Socialism. Yet he is invited to be a Contributing Editor to that paper, and in all radical and liberal circles this defender of plutocracy is regarded as a fellow-worker. He can write that intensely stimulating and ingenious counterblast against feminism, *In Defence of Women*, beside which the scientific efforts of worthy men like Sir Almroth Wright, Belford Bax and Anthony Ludovici are child's play. Their books were violently denounced and abused, whereas his was enthusiastically reviewed, in the leading radical weekly of America, by a militant feminist.

In spite, then, of these temporary alliances Mr. Mencken is alone, for the simple reason that his radical associates have nothing in common with him whatever, beyond their common knowledge that all is not right with the world. The reactionaries, on the other hand, are frightened by his frankness in avowing what they secretly believe, while the vast herd of conservatives who, whatever they may call themselves, constitute the great majority of the American "booboisie"—to borrow his own apt term —imagine that he is a dangerous revolutionary. The latter may be excused on the ground of congenital unsusceptibility to ideas of any kind, and need not detain us. The case of the liberals is more instructive, for they represent a modification of the old simple alignment of H. L. Mencken versus the conservatives, or let us say, "Man versus the Men."

When *The New Republic* published that gorgeous piece of sarcastic humor, "Star-Spangled Men," it was careful to hedge against possible criticism by printing a note disclaiming all agreement with the author, and practically declining editorial responsibility for it. The desire to exploit H. L. Mencken's name and profit by the vigor of his writing, without taking any of the risks presumably attaching to that interesting commentary on war-time manners and morals, was symbolical of his whole relation to the liberal groups in this country. They do not all scuttle for safety when they see him aim his shot, but for practical purposes he can at best serve them merely as a species of *barrage*. Their aims and their ideals are the negation of Mr. Mencken's, for they believe in the plain people, whereas he mistrusts and despises them. If those aims and ideals were realized, his position would be worse than before, since they propose to multiply and extend the machinery through which democracy can make itself felt. By definition democracy can effect nothing that seems desirable to Mr. Mencken. Consequently, the more effective it becomes, the worse it becomes.

"This dominance of mob ways of thinking, this pollution of the whole intellectual life of the country by the prejudices and emotions of the rabble, goes unchallenged because the old landed aristocracy of the colonial era has been engulfed and almost obliterated by the rise of the industrial system, and no new aristocracy has arisen to take its place, and discharge its highly necessary functions. An upper class, of course, exists, but . . . it lacks absolutely anything even remotely resembling an aristocratic point of view. . . . Everywhere else on earth, despite the rise of democracy, an organized minority of aristocrats survives from more spacious days, and . . . it has at least maintained some vestige of its old independence of spirit, and jealously guarded its old right to be heard without risk of penalty. . . . But in the United States it was paralyzed by Jackson and got its death blow from Grant, and since then no successor has been evolved. Thus there is no organized force to oppose the irrational vagaries of the mob."

Typical of many scattered through his writings, this plea for a privileged, leisure class derives directly and logically from H. L. Mencken's individualism, and it differentiates his criticism of American conditions from that of the radicals with whom his name is erroneously associated. The latter are entangled in economic and social theories which have evolved out of the circumstances of European life and have no application whatever to the United States. There is no reason to suppose that this country, having already jumped many links in the European chain, will not develop so differently that no foreign theories will fit the case. The breakdown of capitalism in Europe is, even now, much more than a plausible hypothesis. In America the absence of all the factors which are bringing that about is too obvious for argument. Where Bernard Shaw denounces the Idle Rich, an American Socialist might well denounce the Active Rich, who work without the compulsion of necessity, who encumber positions that might be filled by competent persons in need of earning their livelihood, who do not understand the duties of idleness.

H. L. Mencken's guess as to the future evolution of the American order is based upon the specific contrast between conditions in the United States and in Europe. It has little to recommend it to that school of liberals whose sociology is compounded of Fabianism and more gas and water: "What I see is a vast horde of inferior men broken, after a hopeless fruitless fight, to the hard, uninspiring labor of the world—a race of slaves superbly regimented and

kept steadily in order by great brigades of propa-
gandists, official optimists, scare-mongers, Great
Thinkers and rev. clergy. And over them a minority
of capitalist overlords, well-fed, well-protected,
highly respected, politely envied, and lavishly sup-
plied with endless stores of picture postcards, gaso-
line, silk underwear, mayonnaise, Pontet Canet, toilet
soap and phonograph records."

The characteristic hyperbole is here, but, as usual,
elementary facts are back of Mr. Mencken's words.
"On the evening of the same day that an American
Legionary has his wages reduced 40 per cent. and
his hours of labor increased 25 per cent.; he goes
out at his own risk and expense and helps to tar
and feather some visionary who tries to convince him
he has been swindled." The picture is simply a
news item from the daily paper. "Meanwhile the
Supreme Court of New York decides formally that
'the courts . . . must stand at all times as the rep-
resentatives of capital,' and the newspapers com-
mend the dictum in lavish terms." Once more, a
familiar fact, the evocation of which must awaken
a feeling of recognition in every American breast.
The American people may be democrats, but they
are capitalists to a man, and are as secure from the
contamination of economic heresies as the French
peasant from the wiles of land nationalizers. Hence
the absurdity of the hysterics in high circles whenever some barbarous European tries to communi-
cate his doubts. Hence the even greater absurdity

of those who believe so trustingly that such doubts ought and can be communicated.

"The typical American of to-day has lost all the love of liberty that his forefathers had, and all their distrust of emotion, and pride in self-reliance. He is led no longer by Davy Crocketts; he is led by cheer leaders, press agents, word-mongers, uplifters." Mr. Mencken argues from this fact that the capitalist system is more secure in the United States and will last longer than in Europe. A European would admit the conclusion, but, remembering that economic power precedes political power, he would reverse the order of the syllogism. The United States represents the capitalist ideal, raised to the nth degree of power and efficiency, therefore "the typical American" is all that Mr. Mencken describes him; therefore capitalism is relatively secure. The illusion of political power, of course, has made this possible, for nothing has been added to the romantic eighteenth-century conception of liberty as a purely political idea. Give every man a vote, and deliver him from the obligation of respecting his superiors, symbolized in Europe by "the king business" and the use of the word "Sir," and the rest follows. The country is new and comparatively unexploited; every citizen is potentially a millionaire, as the popular magazines assure him, while the highest offices in the land are not the monopoly of a class.

Mr. Mencken has never traced the obvious relationship between the lack of "Davy Crocketts" and the mercantilism of the Manchester School variety which has flourished here unchallenged from the beginning of the industrial era. Many of the parades at which he laughs are merely advertising devices, as the drums or flags bearing the name of benevolent firms indicate; dervishes of the Billy Sunday type are simply a more spectacular example of the strike-breaking properties of evangelical Christianity; the subsidies which helped the work of the Anti-Saloon League came from the well-filled coffers of people who, not only believed, but openly said, that their Robots would produce more, at no increase in wages, if deprived of alcohol. The connection between American "goose-stepping," as H. L. Mencken calls it, and business is patent. Every one of these manifestations of the herd spirit directly increases the profits of some trade or trades, whether it be the straw hats which are donned irrespective of the weather, the flowers and candies commemorating Mother's Day, the bond drives of the late War, or the incredible antics of village idiots in Tennessee.

Publicity and advertising account for the virulence of most of the pests with which Mr. Mencken is concerned. Hinterland peasants in Europe may believe that the earth is flat, or that the moon is made of green cheese, but no first-rate newspaper troubles to report the matter. Teetotalers describe the horrors of liquor, but their audiences are recruited from little Bethel and their fame is restricted to that audience. Straw hat manufacturers are just as anxious as their American colleagues to sell their products, but they have not the economic power to issue ukases, and must depend upon the weather and the free choice of their customers. If there were any self-constituted organization in London like the Society for the Suppression of Vice, backed by magnates as powerful as those who support Mr. Sumner, Mr. Dreiser and Mr. Cabell would not have escaped there any more than they did here. Europe is far behind the United States, as every Rotarian knows, in the arts of publicity and advertising; the press agent is unknown; the "public relations counsel" would be laughed at. It is not for nothing that the herd stampedes more easily and more often here than there.

H. L. Mencken, however, is authentically American in his indifference to this phenomenon. He has the national capacity for realizing that a gold-brick is being sold, yet admiring the skill of the swindle, and contributing thereby to its success. "My money," he writes, "is laid upon the plutocracy. It will win because it will be able, in the long run, to enlist the finer intelligences. The mob and its maudlin causes attract only sentimentalists and scoundrels, chiefly the latter. . . . The plutocracy can recruit measurably more respectable janissaries, if only because it can make self-interest less obviously costly to *amour-propre*. Its defect and its weakness lie in the fact that it is still too young to have acquired dignity. . . . One seldom finds it undertaking one of its characteristic imbecilities without offering a sonorous moral reason; it spends almost as much to support the Y.M.C.A., vice-crusading, Prohibition and other such puerilities as it spends upon Congressmen, strike-breakers, gunmen, kept patriots and newspapers."

Here it almost seems as if the relation of cause and effect, that is of commercialism and mobocracy, was being proclaimed in its true order. The plutocracy, it seems, spends money on Prohibition, vice-crusading and so forth. Surely, then, one cannot argue that these things are the natural expression of "democracy"? They are determined by the economic power of those who desire to impose them, not by any incurable desire on the part of the proletariat to be reformed. Democracy in France is untroubled by vice-crusaders and teetotalism. Why? Clearly because the economic interests of the country conflict with those blessings, not because that most bourgeois and sedate of races is immoral. In England, where "good form" combines with economic advantage, Lady Astor discovers that her attempts to introduce American political methods are rebuffed by Conservative and Labor governments alike. Apparently the responses of "democracy" to certain stimuli are not entirely unrelated to the ideals and conventions of the governing class. In the United States that class is essentially commercial and plutocratic, and the plain people aspire to be the same. Consequently, they recognize the tunes which their pipers call and dance accordingly.

Assuming that the peculiar manifestations of American "democracy" are not the cause but the effect of the prevailing standards, does this reversal of his reasoning invalidate H. L. Mencken's position? Hardly; save in so far as it restricts the interest and, to a large extent, the validity of his criticism of democracy to this country. In the struggle of capital and labor he sees "two inferiorities" fighting for "the privilege of polluting the world." In his American innocence of economic fundamentals, his view of society in purely political terms, he asks: "What actual difference does it make to a civilized man, when there is a steel strike, whether the workmen win or the mill-owners win? The conflict can interest him only as a spectacle, as the conflict between Bonaparte and the old order in Europe interested Goethe and Beethoven. The victor, whichever way it goes, will simply bring chaos nearer, and so set the stage for a genuine revolution later on, with (let us hope) a new feudalism or something better coming out of it, and a new Thirteenth Century at dawn."

A nation which has escaped the boons of the Thirteenth Century, when, as Schopenhauer said, "fists were more exercised than brains," might as well cherish this notion as the notion that all would be well in a Marxian Utopia. Practically considered, however, the answer to Mr. Mencken's query depends upon who are the owners and who the strikers. In the United States the two sides may be indistinguishable in their common belief in total immersion or the authenticity of Genesis, and in their determination to fleece the public. Elsewhere the alignment is not always so simple, for the strikers might, if they were Fabian Socialists, have a plan for nationalizing steel, which would diminish the costs of production, and nip in the bud a number of embryo millionaires, who would, otherwise, one day have the economic power to prohibit or impose, as their superstitions directed. Where the plutocracy can and does enlist "the finer intelligences" the outcome of a strike, or an election, or any other public issue, will naturally be different from the outcome in a country where "the finer intelligences" are either not enlisted or actively hostile.

H. L. Mencken, however, the most devoted of all Americans in his exclusively national preoccupations, answers his question in terms of American philosophy. In a nation of small capitalists and trusts, it is absurd to look for economic ideas which do not rest upon the idea of profiteering, to use in its original meaning a word which has become distorted since it was first coined by the advocates of National Guilds in the London *New Age*. Profiteering is not the making of exceptional profits; a profiteer is one who cannot conceive of production for any other purpose but profit. He is not only Judge Gary and John D. Rockefeller, he is every one of the million victims of New York's subways, who listen without a smile to the theory that transit in that city is being run at a loss. In other words the assumption that the object in view is not the transportation of human beings but the earning of dividends. Mr. Mencken's support of plutocracy is not only logical, but it inevitably follows from the great American premise of economic individualism. He expounds the national philosophy, as he said of Bernard Shaw, in terms of the scandalous.

Walt Whitman's: "Produce fine people, the rest follows"; Jefferson's: "That government is best which governs least," are the two themes upon which H. L. Mencken has embroidered. His essay "On Government," is simply a variation upon Emerson's plea that "the less government we have, the better—the fewer laws, the less confided power." With Thoreau he laments that "the American has dwindled into an Odd Fellow,—one who may be known by the development of his organ of gregariousness, and a manifest lack of intellect and cheerful self-reliance." Lincoln anticipated his discourses upon politicians, when he declared that "politicians are a set of men who have interests aside from the interests of the people and who . . . are, taken as a mass, at least one long step removed from honest men." So intensely does he cling to this old-fashioned Americanism that one must go back in the annals, literary and political, for any trace of the same spirit.

Here and there, until the Department of Justice jailed or deported them, were a few ingenuous Socialists, who quoted the Declaration of Independence, gazed with moist eyes upon the Statue of Liberty, and cited the Bill of Rights. They were—either literally or metaphorically—alien elements in the body politic, which was drastically purged, and was much relieved by their disappearance. H. L. Mencken suffered no such indignities because his enthusiasm for those interesting, if now somewhat pathetic relics of Anglo-Saxon idealism, was autochthonous. He has the American virtue of pragmatism: whatever "works" is right. At all events, acquiescence is more sensible than revolt. The misguided Debs quotes the Declaration of Independence because he believes in it, and he is promptly clubbed by a freedom-loving Irish policeman. Mr. Mencken quotes it because he thinks it is nonsense, and the authorities recognize in him a man and a brother.

He defines his attitude quite frankly in the third series of *Prejudices*, where he postulates the choice of having to resist or submit to the exactions of a stupid majority. "I shall get converted to their nonsense instantly, and so retire to safety with my right thumb laid against my nose and my fingers waving like wheat in the wind. . . . What, after all, is one more lie?" This, at bottom, is the modern American method of meeting a situation which would elsewhere provoke instant revolt. Where a true-born Briton rebels and writes to *The Times* to pro-

test, an American laughs and says: "I can fix it."
The one relies on immediate resistance, the other
upon his conviction that there are ways and means
of getting round most difficulties. The one has the
right of free speech; the other has Prohibition.
Both are presumably happy, but the American seems
to be unaware that his complaints and protesta-
tions, of which he is prodigal after the event, should
have been energetic and effective beforehand, when
they might have really helped. This attitude is perfectly comprehensible in America, for it is a muti-
lated remnant of the old sturdy individualism. The
power of self-assertion is gone, atrophied, but the
purely individualistic egotism, which says: every
man for himself, remains. So it is "up to" the other
fellow to resist, if he wants to. With the result that
all find themselves in the same quandary, in the end,
as no concerted action has been taken based on instinctive resistance.

H. L. Mencken's philosophy, therefore, in all its
elements is thoroughly American. He represents the
old order of sentimental individualism, with its sus-
picion of government, its faith in personal effort, its
optimistic good humor. As he himself has shown,
that spirit has waned in America under the pressure
of industrialism, so that, as its extant spokesman
he has an air of novelty, which frightens his more
stupid opponents but actually explains his appeal
to his more intelligent countrymen. They realize
that he is as remote from Prussianism as Abe Lin-

coln, that he is no revolutionary, but the most articulate and aggressive expression of unspoiled Americanism. "I am, in many fields, a flouter of the accepted revelation and hence immoral, but the field of economics is not one of them. Here, indeed, I know of no man who is more orthodox than I am. I believe that the present organization of society, as bad as it is, is better than any other that has ever been proposed. . . . I am in favor of free competition in all human enterprises, and to the utmost limit, I admire successful scoundrels, and shrink from all Socialists. . . ."

This is indigenous iconoclasm. No other country to-day could produce it. It is as far removed from the realities of this age as the Declaration of Independence. This sort of heresy is "the apex of normalcy."

THE CRITIC

IN stressing the orthodoxy of Henry Louis
Mencken, Baltimore householder and genial com-
panion at the *Stammtisch*, hard-working hedonist
and champion of the plutocracy, romantic survivor
of the age of American innocence,—in this view of
him as an American of the old allegiance to individualism, the aim has been to dissociate the man
from the legend, and by his own words to demon-
strate the authenticity of his Americanism. This
seemed to be necessary because of the legend in question, and because of the popular misconceptions
based thereon. "In the United States," as he says,
"I am commonly held suspect as a foreigner. . . .
Abroad, especially in England, I am sometimes put
to the torture for my intolerable Americanism."
These two views have determined the character of
this analysis so far.

Mr. Mencken holds that "the two views are less
far apart than they seem to be. The fact is that
I am superficially so American in ways of speech and
thought, that the foreigner is deceived, whereas the
native, more familiar with the true signs, sees that
under the surface there is incurable antagonism to
most of the ideas that Americans hold to be sound."
Here, of course, the author is simply engaged in

fostering the legend.   He ignores the unanimous agreement of the American critics who have really understood him,—Vincent O'Sullivan, Burton Rascoe and Edmund Wilson, for example—that he is "as peculiarly American as pumpkin-pie or a Riker-Hegeman drugstore," to quote Mr. O'Sullivan.   As Mr. Rascoe points out, "this delusion of un-Americanism on the part of Americans who have risen above the mob is common enough."   In other words, not only is it essential to an understanding of Mr. Mencken that his fundamental American orthodoxy should be established, but the very necessity for establishing it is part of his Americanism. No European writer would think that he had denied his nationality by holding opinions in which there was "an incurable antagonism to most of the ideas" which his compatriots held to be sound.   Nor would the accusation be made.   By accepting it, Mr. Mencken proves once more how completely his mentality is colored by his nationality.

Now, however, we come to the point where H. L. Mencken must be considered, not in relation to the ideas which, however disguised, are part of the American *Weltanschauung*, but in relation to those ideas which brought him into immediate conflict with his contemporaries.   As we have seen, from 1899 until 1916 his activities were local, and it was mainly as a critic of literature, through his articles in *The Smart Set*, that he reached the general public outside Baltimore.   In that capacity he not only caused the mobilization of his opponents, but also attracted that small but solid phalanx of supporters and admirers, with and through whom his influence spread. He is now so familiar an American figure, his public is so large, that few people realize the relative obscurity in which he lived until recently. In 1917 he published *A Book of Prefaces*, and that date marks the beginning of his rise to popular fame. The shock of the War precipitated events by providing him with an audience prematurely ripe to receive his ideas and an enormous field in which to expend energies previously concentrated upon the affairs of Maryland. Mr. Carl Van Doren, with his first-hand knowledge of the educational world, testifies that "no other contemporary critic is so well known in the colleges. No other is so influential amongst the latest generation of boys and girls of letters."

The explanation of Mr. Mencken's fame as a heretic lies in the circumstances of his career as a literary critic rather than in his achievement as a pioneer of Shavianism and Nietzscheanism—of Ibsenism, too, for in 1909, in collaboration with a Baltimore friend, Holger A. Koppel, he translated *Little Eyolf*, *A Doll's House*, *Ghosts*, *Hedda Gabler* and *An Enemy of the People*, of which only the first two have been published. Nowadays it is difficult to believe that the criticism which editors so eagerly invite and publishers rejoice to quote was regarded as heretical. It rarely appeared outside the pages of Mr. Mencken's own magazine, and was boycotted, as

a rule, save when some irate pedagogue burst into
hysterical denunciation. In the backwoods the same
shrill vociferations may still be heard. In this connection Mr. Mencken's quotations from a "Texas
Taine," named Doughty, in the fourth series of
Prejudices, may be referred to the curious.

What currently passed for intelligent comment on
Mr. Mencken may be seen in such essays as that
written by Stuart P. Sherman in *The Nation,* when
A Book of Prefaces appeared. This work, unlike
the later volumes of *Prejudices,* is devoted exclusively to literature: studies of Joseph Conrad, Theodore Dreiser and James Huneker, with "Puritanism
as a Literary Force" by way of conclusion. This
final chapter may be read as the best summary of all
that Mr. Mencken set out to combat as a critic of
American literature. Its thesis is so simple and so
true that it is elementary: the "moral obsession has
given a strong color to American literature," that
the aim of a work of imagination is not the promo-
tion of virtue, and that, so long as ethical rather
than esthetic considerations dominate American
criticism, there can be no great art in America. As
is his habit, Mr. Mencken substantiates his points
and illustrates his arguments by quoting specific
cases, among others that of Theodore Dreiser and
the notorious history of *The 'Genius,'* as to which
his contentions have since been upheld by the courts.

One might differ from Mr. Mencken's estimate of

Conrad, Dreiser and Huneker, or argue that puritanism is no obstacle to the development of art and literature. But that is not Dr. Sherman's way, and his way is so typical of what Mr. Mencken has had to overcome, that extensive quotation is desirable, if only because from this one specimen may be learnt all that the general body of conservative criticism in America has been able to say in reply to him. Thus Dr. Stuart P. Sherman on "Beautifying American Literature":

"Mr. Mencken is not at all satisfied with life or literature in America, for he is a lover of the beautiful. We have nowadays no beautiful literature in this country with the possible exception of Mr. Dreiser's novels; nor do we seem in a fair way to produce anything esthetically gratifying. Probably the root of our difficulty is that, with the exception of Mr. Huneker, Otto Heller, Ludwig Lewisohn, Mr. Untermeyer, G. S. Viereck, the author of 'Der Kampf um deutsche Kultur in Amerika,' and a few other choice souls, we have no critics who, understanding what beauty is, serenely and purely love it. Devoid of esthetic sense, our native Anglo-Saxon historians cannot even guess what ails our native literature. For a competent historical account of our national anesthesia one should turn, Mr. Mencken assures us, to a translation from some foreign tongue —we cannot guess which—by Dr. Leon Kellner.

"Though a lover of the beautiful, Mr. Mencken is

not a German. He was born in Baltimore, September 12, 1880. That fact should silence the silly people who have suggested that he and Dreiser are the secret agents of the Wilhelmstrasse, 'told off to inject subtle doses of *Kultur* into a naïf and pious people.' Furthermore, Mr. Mencken is, with George Jean Nathan, editor of that stanchly American receptacle for *belles-lettres*, 'The Smart Set'. . . ."

"He is a member of the Germania Männerchor, and he manages to work the names of most of the German musicians into his first three discourses. His favorite philosopher happens to be Nietzsche, whose beauties he has expounded in two books— first the 'philosophy,' then the 'gist' of it. He perhaps a little flauntingly dangles before us the seductive names of Wedekind, Schnitzler, Bierbaum, Schoenberg and Korngold. He exhibits a certain Teutonic gusto in tracing the 'Pilsner motive' through the work of Mr. Huneker. His publisher is indeed Mr. Knopf. But Mr. Knopf disarms anti-German prejudice by informing us that Mr. Mencken is of 'mixed blood—Saxon, Bavarian, Hessian, Irish and English'; or, as Mr. Mencken himself puts it, with his unfailing good taste, he is a 'mongrel.' One cannot therefore understand exactly why Mr. Knopf thinks it valuable to announce that Mr. Mencken 'was in Berlin when relations between Germany and the United States were broken off,' nor why he adds: 'Since then he has done no newspaper work, save a few occasional articles.' Surely there can have been no external interference with Mr. Mencken's purely esthetic ministry to the American people.

"As Mr. Mencken conceives the esthetic ministry, there is nothing in the world more dispassionate, disinterested, freer from moral, religious or political significance. The 'typical American critic,' to be sure, is a pestilent and dangerous fellow; he is a Puritan; he is ever bent on giving instruction in the sphere of conduct; he is always talking about politics and morals. But, Mr. Mencken assures us, 'criticism, as the average American "intellectual" understands it, is what a Frenchman, a German or a Russian would call donkeyism.' Now, though Mr. Mencken is not a German, he has an open mind. One may even say that he has a 'roomy' mind. And by that token he is quite certainly not a typical American critic. We imagine that he may fairly be taken as a representative of the high European critical outlook over 'beautiful letters'—as he loves to call such sensitive work as that of Mr. Dreiser. He does not wander over the wide field of conduct with a birch rod; he simply perceives and feels and interprets the soul of loveliness in art—to use his own expressive phrase, he beats a drum for beauty. . . . Presently one begins to suspect that his quarrel with American criticism is not so much in behalf of beauty as in behalf of a *Kultur* which has been too inhospitably received by such of his fellow citizens as look to another *Stammvater* than his. Of course, the true explanation is that Mr. Mencken's culture

propaganda is what a drummer (for *das Schöne*)
would call his 'side line.' Beauty is the main bur-
den of his pack. . . .

"Mr. Mencken's continuous tirade against everything respectable in American morals, against everything characteristic of American society, and
against everything and everybody distinguished in
American scholarship and letters is not precisely and
strictly *esthetic* criticism; indeed, an unsympathetic
person might say that it is not criticism at all, but
mere scurrility and blackguardism. His continuous
laudation of a Teutonic-Oriental pessimism and
nihilism in philosophy, of anti-democratic politics,
of the subjection and contempt of women, of the
Herrenmoral, and of anything but Anglo-Saxon civilization is not precisely and strictly *esthetic* criticism; an unsympathetic person might call it infatu-
ated propagandism. But, of course, all these things
are properly to be regarded as but the *obiter dicta*
of a quiet drummer for beauty.

"Still, for the esthetic critic, it is a pleasure to
turn from Mr. Mencken's somewhat polemical general ideas to the man himself as revealed by the
subtle and finely woven garment of his style.
Though not a German, Mr. Mencken has a beautiful style; and though he could be a professor
if he would, he has a learned style. To his
erudition let stand as witnesses the number-
less choice words calculated to send the vulgar
reader to a dictionary; 'multipara,' 'chandala,' 'la-

maseries,' 'coryza,' 'lagniappe,' 'umbilicarii,' 'Treuga Dei,' 'swamis,' 'gemaras,' 'munyonic,' 'glycosuria.' This is clearly the vocabulary of an artist and a scholar. As an additional sign of his erudition consider his discovery that Mr. Dreiser 'stems' from the Greeks; also his three-line quotation from a Greek dramatist—in the original Greek. . . .

"The sheer verbal loveliness of writing like this can never pass away. It is the writing of a sensitive, intellectual aristocrat. It has the quality and tone of high breeding. It is the flower and fragrance of a noble and elevated mind that dwells habitually with beauty. Does not one breathe a sigh of relief as one escapes from the ruck and muck of American 'culture' into the clear and spacious atmosphere of genuine esthetic criticism? If by exchanging our American set of standards for his 'European' set we could learn to write as Mr. Mencken does, why do we hesitate? Well, as a matter of fact, there is already a brave little band of sophomores in criticism who do not hesitate. These humming Ephemera are mostly preserved in the pure amber of Mr. Mencken's prose. At everything accepted as finely and soundly American swift fly the pebbles, out gushes the corrosive vapor of a *discriminating* abuse. The prospect for beautiful letters in America is visibly brightening."

In a later essay, reprinted in *Americans*, Dr. Sherman returns to this theme, making great play with the ankles of the young girl who reads Mr. Mencken, and with the "Loyal Independent Order of United

Hiberno-German-Anti-English-Americans," who are his supporters. The conclusion of all this Ku Klux Kriticism is that H. L. Mencken's abominable doctrines have found their appropriate audience, not amongst the Nordic Protestant Americans, but amongst "children whose parents or grandparents brought their copper-kettles from Russia, tilled the soil of Hungary, taught the mosaic-law in Poland, cut Irish turf, ground optical glass in Germany, dispensed Bavarian beer, or fished mackerel around the Skagerrack." Mr. Mencken, in brief, is the prophet of the new America "without cultural inheritance."

In a thousand variations these charges have been brought against H. L. Mencken, ever since the policy of ignoring him was abandoned. His main indictment against American literature and its critics, that they are wholly indifferent to esthetics, has not been seriously questioned. The specific battles waged by him on behalf of writers victimized or neglected because of the puritan obsession have resulted in victories. Theodore Dreiser, Ring Lardner, James Huneker, George Ade, James Branch Cabell, Joseph Hergesheimer, Willa Cather, Eugene O'Neill and Sherwood Anderson are some of the Americans on whose behalf he stormed the citadels of academic conservatism. He was the first editor to print James Joyce in America; Havelock Ellis, Lord Dunsany, Pío Baroja, Ibsen, Hauptmann, Strindberg, Sudermann, Nietzsche and Shaw must be counted amongst the foreigners whom he introduced or helped to wider

fame in this country. His dissection of Thorstein
Veblen is an operation comparable to Shaw's ex-
posure of Max Nordau.

With *Jurgen* and *The 'Genius'* restored to circulation, in defiance of the professional moralists, and
every author for whom he seriously fought now accepted by all educated Americans, H. L. Mencken
can afford to smile at the sound and fury still per-
ceptible in the camp of his enemies. At the outset
of his career, he tells us, "an ancient" advised him
to make whatever he had to say interesting, "to write
a good story. . . . If you want to read Lessing and
Freytag, Hazlitt and Brunetière, go read them: they
will do you no harm. . . . But unless you can make
people *read* your criticisms, you may as well shut up
your shop, and the only way to make them read
you is to give them something exciting." Sometimes
this could be accomplished "with a bladder on a
string, usually with a meat-ax." The essential thing
was to "knock somebody on the head every day."
Mr. Mencken began to act on this advice and "whenever I acted upon it," he confesses, "I found that
it worked." Here he frankly explains the method
which, in its turn, explains why so much indignation
preceded his final assault upon the old régime in
American criticism.

"When I first began to practice as a critic, in
1908, . . . it was a time of almost inconceivable
complacency and conformity. Hamilton Wright
Mabie was still alive and still taken seriously, and all

the young pedagogues who aspired to the critical gown imitated him in his watchful stupidity. This camorra had delivered a violent wallop to Dreiser eight years before, and he was yet suffering from his bruises . . . the American novelists most admired by most publishers, by most readers and by all practicing critics were Richard Harding Davis, Robert W. Chambers and James Lane Allen. . . . To-day, it seems to me, the American imaginative writer, whether he be novelist, poet or dramatist, is quite as free as he deserves to be. He is free to depict the life about him precisely as he sees it, and to interpret it in any manner he pleases . . . the importance and puissance of comstockery, I believe, is quite as much overestimated as the importance and puissance of the objurgations still hurled at sense and honesty by the provincial professors of American Idealism, the Genius of America and other such phantasms."

In this retrospect Mr. Mencken refrains from suggesting the important part which his own writings have played in bringing about the change. He again pays his tribute to Theodore Dreiser, to his example, his staunchness of purpose, and his importance as a rallying point. He would not be human if he had failed to indulge in a sardonic laugh at the expense of the "alfalfa *Gelehrten*" who whooped for *Babbitt*, "apparently on the theory that praising Lewis would make the young of the national species forget Dreiser." Perhaps one ought to add, or forget their amazing persecution of Dreiser. "The important thing is that, despite the caterwauling of the Comstocks and the pedagogues, a reasonable freedom for the serious artist now prevails—that publishers stand ready to print him, that critics exist who are competent to recognize him and willing to do battle for him."

This essay in *Prejudices: Fourth Series* will repay reading for its excellent summary of all that has been accomplished under the stimulus of H. L. Mencken's influence and that of the writers who aided him, or who responded to his ever generous encouragement. Of that encouragement Burton Rascoe has justly said: "He early established a sort of personal relationship with every promising writer in the country. . . . I have yet to meet a man under thirty-five with articulate ideas who has not a sheaf of those lively, hearty notes whereby Mencken conveys a maximum of good cheer and boisterous comment within a minimum of space." Disingenuous efforts have been made to controvert Mr. Mencken's account of the literary hierarchy with which he was confronted, but the names substituted for those he mentions are all names more honored to-day than in 1908. Once again Mr. Mencken is correct as to his facts.

The position of H. L. Mencken has also been modified by the passage of those years which he passes under review. As a relief from the patriotic innuendoes and appeals to race prejudice of Dr. Sherman and others, the moral exhortations and the academic snobberies, we may turn to the actual criticism of Mr. Mencken by the generation that reads and understands him. Mr. Rascoe's "Notes for an Epitaph," which appeared in *The Literary Review* of *The New York Evening Post*, in 1922, provides a retrospect and a contrast which are instructive and agreeable.

Mr. Rascoe confesses his surprise when, in 1921, H. L. Mencken appeared among the writers for *The New Republic*, became a Contributing Editor to *The Nation*, and was honored by the publication of his photograph in the fashionable magazines alongside Dr. Frank Crane, Arthur Brisbane and Charlie Chaplin, "With startling suddenness he who had been without the pale for so long was quoted everywhere with approval. His praise of the *Liberator* and the *Yale Review* was seized upon by the editors as valuable advertising copy. . . . The *Freeman* and the *Bookman*, the *New York Evening Post* and the *New York Times* scattered among their discourses the pungent observations of the sage of Baltimore. For twelve years or more he had been writing about books and not a single publisher had ever had the temerity to quote his opinions in advertisements. Now he is quoted more often than Willian Lyon Phelps.

"Thus in a brief space, was Mencken brought into the line of regimented thought. . . . He no longer shouts and pounds the table. His hat is no longer askew. . . . One recalls with a sardonic smile that only a short time ago Mencken was performing premature obsequies for the late James Huneker because Huneker's 'work in *Punch,* the *Times,* and the *Sun* shows an unaccustomed acquiescence in current valuation' . . . for Mencken's 'acquiescence' is even more complete. He praises such youthful masterpieces as 'The Beginning of Wisdom'; he has been the subject of a critical appreciation by one of the kept-idealists of the *New Republic;* he gags a bit at D. H. Lawrence; he actually makes a gingerly curtsey to his ancient enemy, Stuart P. Sherman, an Urbana professor. . . . He is acquiring years; he is in the unhappy position of a born disputant who finds no one to disagree with him."

This perfectly accurate account of Mr. Mencken's present situation presents obvious discrepancies from Dr. Sherman's picture of him as the leader of an uncultivated rabble of brachycephalic *déracinés.* The *jeune fille,* whose legs obsess the author of *Americans,* is not the person by whom one tests the effects of Mr. Mencken's ideas. "His admirers," Mr. Rascoe continues, "still love him; but more than one is at work on his epitaph. Nowadays you will not see Van Wyck Brooks, or John Macy or John Peale Bishop or Ben Hecht or F. Scott Fitzgerald refer to him in print without certain reservations; as a literary critic, they intimate, he leaves something to be desired. Only the oldsters, who are just becoming aware of him, hold him to be infallible. . . . Mencken is too conservative in his literary judgments to satisfy a growing audience in this country with catholic taste and inquisitive habits of mind. . . . The truth is that the literary generation now gaining recognition has progressed beyond the reaches of Mencken's esthetic equipment."

Mr. Rascoe has here drawn attention to a fact which must become increasingly more obvious as the younger writers develop. It is a fact, moreover, which contrasts dramatically with the illusions both of the belated friends no less than the old-established enemies of H. L. Mencken. While the latter are still denouncing him as a suborner of youth, the objects of their misplaced concern are discussing him quite rationally, if not always impartially. Mr. Rascoe himself seems to share one of their chief errors— probably a natural reaction against Mr. Mencken's deliberate suppression of scholarly allusion—when he says: "There is meager evidence in the whole body of his critical work that he has read any book published before 1880. With the cultural heritage of all nations, excepting only the English Bible, he reflects little intimacy." In return for this, we have now to suffer a sophomoric school of premature pundits who display the learning of which most civilized men are conscious only during the first rapturous years of their 'teens.

Mr. Mencken himself is not unaware of the change both in himself and his public; he has hinted that his function as a literary critic has been fully discharged. "I moved steadily from practical journalism, with its dabblings in politics, economics and so on, towards purely esthetic concerns, chiefly literature and music, but of late I have felt a strong pull in the other direction, and what interest me chiefly to-day is what may be called public psychology, *i.e.*, the nature of the ideas that the larger masses of men hold, and the processes whereby they reach them. If I do any serious writing hereafter, it will be in that field." The founding of *The American Mercury* in 1924, showed the new trend of Mr. Mencken's interests, for *belles-lettres* have been relegated to the background, and both his editorials and his critical articles have been concerned with ideas rather than with pure literature.

While he undoubtedly owes his fame largely to his work as a literary critic, H. L. Mencken's gradual abandonment of this field is not surprising. Had conditions in 1908 been what they are to-day, it is open to doubt whether he would have turned his energies in that direction at all. What attracted him was the opportunity, the necessity, for a struggle with the forces that were stifling the growth of art and literature in this country, rather than any desire to impose a theory of criticism. His actual conception of the critic's function has always been self-contradictory, and his doctrinal pronouncements have been destructively analyzed and severely criticized from the most varied standpoints, from the

Crocean J. E. Spingarn to the Marxian V. F. Calverton. All that remains constant is his practice, which has been to insist upon freedom for the artist, upon such conditions as alone can ensure the recognition of creative originality.

The only art which Mr. Mencken has viewed without regard for its intellectual content, is music. Here, and here only, does his writing become emotional; at times, sentimental. The creator of music stands highest in his scale of artistic values, and to music alone he has responded with his whole being, revealing himself, of course, as the great conservative that he really is. He is as contemptuous of jazz and musical comedy as a Paul Elmer More might be of George Ade, and his preferences, Brahms, Bach, Beethoven, Schumann, Haydn, have their equivalent in the predilection of the college professors for the authors of the Five-foot Bookshelf.

As a humorist of the first rank, H. L. Mencken has not yet received his due. He combines that essential element in American humor, grotesque exaggeration, with an intellectual quality which is absent from almost all authors popularly regarded as humorous. *A Book of Burlesques* is as thoroughly American as anything of Mark Twain's, but it lacks his incurable vulgarity and cheap philistinism, as it is free from the sheer puerility which renders the popular American funny man so intolerable to the uninitiated. Here one does not find "ancient and infantile wheezes, as flat to the taste as so many crystals of hyposulphite of soda," to quote his own description of a widely acclaimed humorist of to-day. Mr. Mencken's humor is informed by a genuine comic spirit, which has just that tang of intelligence whose absence explains the ephemeral reputations of most writers in the depressing limbo reserved for the professional humorists of yesteryear. Both his sense of humor and his instinctive love of patient pedantry are revealed in the portentous tome, *The American Language*, which "grew out of a satirical article on American grammar, written for the Baltimore *Evening Sun* in 1910 or thereabout." His reward was ample when the inevitable agitation stirred the minds of the Colonials, and one of them described this study of the vulgar tongue as "a wedge to split asunder the two great English-speaking peoples." Whether one accept or reject the theory based upon this voluminous evidence of the existence of an American vulgate, it is obviously unnecessary to accuse Mr. Mencken of having invented that tongue. The Americanism surely antedates even the reign of this Anti-Christ, and all that he can properly be charged with is having expended a vast amount of time, learning and research in tracing its growth and development. His versions of the Gettysburg address and the Declaration of Independence in the vernacular are masterpieces of Menckenian satire.

This book, to conclude, is typical of H. L. Mencken and all his works. Whatever his ostensible subject, in whichever one of the varied fields of his varied and restless activity, his method and aim are the same. He chose his objective at the outset of his career and he has never deviated from it. A born individualist and iconoclast, his multifarious criticism has tended to strike in all directions at such beliefs, superstitions, laws and conventions as threaten the growth of free personality. When Nietzsche and Ibsen and Shaw could be effectively employed to clear the ground of social and political rubble, he used them. Theodore Dreiser served as a standard under which he could honorably call the intelligent to arms against the defenders of inert tradition. The American language was simply one amongst a host of other phenomena, positive and negative, to which attention must be called, if there was to be any realistic conception of the actual America of to-day as distinct from that of the dreams of New England.

Mr. Mencken, for all that his enemies may say, has shown throughout his lifetime a more consistent and exclusive concern for purely American problems than any other public figure in this country above the level of a politician. He has contrived to escape most of the temptations which beset men of his type, once they have caught the public ear, because, as he once said, "the difference between a moral man and a man of honor is that the latter regrets a discreditable act, even when it has worked and he has not been caught." If his judgments

sometimes confirm the philistines in their contempt
for art which they do not understand, and if his
pragmatic dogma concerning the ease and importance of achieving material success adds further
weight to the prevailing mercantilism—these things
are not due to any deliberate attempt on his part to
play down to the facile prejudices of his audience.
They come, as has been shown, from the deep-seated
and natural identity of his fundamental philosophy
with that of his national environment.

"Of a piece with the absurd pedagogical demand
for so-called constructive criticism is the doctrine
that an iconoclast is a hollow and evil fellow unless
he prove his case. Why, indeed, should he prove it?
Doesn't he prove enough when he proves by his
blasphemy that this or that idol is defectively con-
vincing—that at least *one* visitor to the shrine is
left full of doubts? . . . The pedant and the priest
have always been the most expert logicians—and the
most diligent disseminators of nonsense and worse.
The liberation of the human mind has never been
furthered by such learned dunderheads; it has been
furthered by gay fellows who heaved dead cats into
sanctuaries and then went roistering down the high-
ways of the world, proving to all men that doubt,
after all, was safe—that the god in the sanctuary
was finite in his power, and hence a fraud."

From one who declares himself "wholly devoid of
public spirit or moral purpose" this may be taken
as a confession of faith. It clarifies the purpose

behind all the wit, humor, boisterous gayety and mocking laughter, which H. L. Mencken invests his criticism of American life. "One horse-laugh is worth ten thousand syllogisms," he says, and we remember that Swift and Voltaire still live to prove it. "The only thing I respect is intellectual honesty, of which, of course, intellectual courage is a necessary part. A Socialist who goes to jail for his opinions seems to me a much finer man than the judge who sends him there, though I disagree with all the ideas of the Socialist and agree with some of those of the judge." Thus the American libertarian joins hands with his eighteenth-century French forbear who said: "I am opposed to every one of your beliefs but will uphold to the end your right to express them."

BIBLIOGRAPHY

Ventures into Verse. Baltimore, 1903.
George Bernard Shaw: His Plays. Boston, 1905.
The Philosophy of Friedrich Nietzsche. Boston, 1908.
The Artist. A Drama without Words. Boston, 1912.
A Book of Burlesques. New York, 1916.
A Little Book in C Major. New York, 1916.
A Book of Prefaces. New York, 1917.
Damn! A Book of Calumny. New York, 1918.
In Defense of Women. New York, 1918.
The American Language. New York, 1919.
Prejudices: First Series. New York, 1919.
Prejudices: Second Series. New York, 1920.
Prejudices: Third Series. New York, 1922.
Prejudices: Fourth Series. New York, 1924.

IN COLLABORATION

Men *versus* the Man. (With R. R. La Monte.) New York, 1910.
Europe after 8.15. (With George Jean Nathan and Willard Huntington Wright.) New York, 1914.
Pistols for Two. (With George Jean Nathan.) New York, 1917.
Heliogabalus: A Buffoonery in Three Acts. (With George Jean Nathan.) New York, 1920.
The American Credo. (With George Jean Nathan.) New York, 1920.

EDITED WITH INTRODUCTIONS

The Players' Ibsen. A Doll's House. Boston, 1909.
The Players' Ibsen. Little Eyolf. Boston, 1909.
The Gist of Nietzsche. Boston, 1910.
Ventures in Common Sense. By E. W. Howe. New York, 1919.
Youth and Egolatry. By Pío Baroja. New York, 1920.
The Antichrist. By F. W. Nietzsche. New York, 1920.
We Moderns. By Edwin Muir. New York, 1920.
Democracy and the Will to Power. By James N. Wood. New York, 1921.
In Defense of Women. By H. L. Mencken. New York, 1922.
(The last six titles form the series of Free Lance Books.)

MORE IMPORTANT MISCELLANEA

Blanchette and The Escape: Two Plays by Brieux. Boston, 1913. Contains a Preface.
The Master Builder. Pillars of Society. Hedda Gabler. By Henrik Ibsen. New York, 1918. Contains an Introduction.
The Profession of Journalism. Edited by Willard Grosvenor Bleyer, Ph.D. Boston, 1918. Contains "Newspaper Morals."
On American Books. Edited by Francis Hackett. New York, 1920. Contains "The Literary Capital of the United States."
The Line of Love. By James Branch Cabell. New York, 1921. Contains an Introduction.
Civilization in the United States. Edited by Harold Stearns. New York, 1922. Contains "Politics."

These United States. Edited by Ernest Gruening. First
Series. New York, 1923. Contains "Maryland,
Apex of Normalcy."
Criticism in America. New York, 1924. Contains
"Footnote on Criticism."
For a complete list of pamphlets and contributions to
books see "A Bibliography of the Writings of H. L.
Mencken," by Carroll Frey, published at Philadelphia,
in 1924, by the Centaur Book Shop.

THE END